Why We Have Evening

Why We Have Evening

Poems by Leonard Orr

Cherry Grove Collections

© 2010 by Leonard Orr

Published by Cherry Grove Collections
P.O. Box 541106
Cincinnati, OH 45254-1106

ISBN: 9781934999905
LCCN: 2010924258

Poetry Editor: Kevin Walzer
Business Editor: Lori Jareo

Visit us on the web at www.cherry-grove.com

Acknowledgments

The following poems in *Why We Have Evening* appear in my chapbook collection, *Daytime Moon* (Kanona NY: FootHills Publishing, 2005): "Clouders," "My Way with Planets," "Cyclic," "Nettles," "Asking," "Thin Man in the Bathroom Mirror," "Security," "Hours and Hours and Hours," "Aftereffects," "Reading," "Purity of Essence," "In Your Absence," "Papers," "Thanksgiving," "Psychosomatic," "Sun and Wheat Fields," "Yoga Practice," "Japanese Style," "Snow Flocking, Signs of Solstice," "Permeable," "Poem for Lunch," "These Are My Crustacean Days," "Keep This Between Us," "I Thought About You All Day While I Worked," "Daytime Moon, Shifts of Season," "The Meaning of Salmon," "Limitations of Guidebooks," and "Wind Farms." I am very grateful to the publisher, Michael Czarnecki, for his work on the volume.

"Clouders" was published in *Black Warrior Review* (Spring, 2004). It was also published in the anthology *Mute Note Earthward*, edited by Stephen Roxborough (Seattle: Reischling Press, 2004).

"Security" was published in *Poetry Midwest* (Winter, 2006).

"Reading" was published in the British journal *Obsessed with Pipework* (2001) and was reprinted in *Tattoos on Cedar*, edited by Stephen Roxborough (Seattle: Washington Poets Association, 2006).

"Papers" was published in *Poetry East*, 53 (Fall, 2004).

"Psychosomatic" was published in *Poetry East*, 52 (Spring, 2004).

"Sun and Wheatfields" and "The Shortest Distance" were published in *poemeleon* 1.2 (Winter, 2006).

"Snow Flocking, Signs of Solstice" and "Snoqualmie Pass" were published in *Crab Creek Review* 20.1 (Spring/Summer, 2006).

"Family History" was published in *Fugue* 31 (Summer-Fall, 2006).

"Tales of the Cruise" was published in *Writing on the Edge* 14.1 (Fall, 2003).

"Poem for Lunch" was published in *Rosebud* 25 (Fall, 2002) as a runner-up for the William Stafford Prize for Poetry. It was published in *Pontoon* 6 (2003) and reprinted in the 10th anniversary edition, *Pontoon* 10 (2008).

"Keep This Between Us" was published in *Poetry International* 9 (2004).

"I Thought About You All Day While I Worked" and "Yiddish for Travelers" were published in the 2007 *Voices Israel Anthology* edited by Helen Bar-Lev.

"The Meaning of Salmon" was published in *Bellowing Ark* 18.3 (2002).

"Grieving" was published in *Midstream* (Nov./Dec., 2004).

"Wind Farms" was published in *Rosebud* 31 (December, 2004), as a runner-up for the William Stafford Poetry Award.

"Unsent Postcards from Unknown Cities" was published in *Orbis* 138 (Nov., 2006).

"Completely" was published in *Poetry East* 59-59 (Spring, 2007).

"Leap Second" was published in *Isotope: A Journal of Literary Nature and Science Writing* 6.1 (Spring/Summer, 2008).

"Dried Fruit on Ben Yehuda Street" was published in *Poetry International* 12 (2008).

"Always Night These Days," "How to Adore," and "Winter Drive to Pullman" were published in *Pontoon* 10 (2008).

"Tel Aviv" was published in *Natural Bridge* 20 (Fall, 2008).

Table of Contents

Clouders ... 13
My Way with Planets ... 14
Cyclic ... 15
Nettles ... 16
Asking ... 17
Thin Man in the Bathroom Mirror ... 18
Security ... 19
Hours and Hours and Hours ... 20
Aftereffects ... 21
Reading ... 23
Purity of Essence ... 24
In Your Absence ... 25
Papers ... 26
Thanksgiving ... 27
Psychosomatic ... 28
Tel Aviv ... 29
Sun and Wheatfields ... 30
Spring Planting ... 32
Yoga Practice ... 33
Japanese Style ... 35
Snow Flocking, Signs of Solstice ... 36
Permeable ... 37
Family History ... 38
Tales of the Cruise ... 39
Poem for Lunch ... 40
These Are My Crustacean Days ... 41
Monet's *The Magpie* ... 42
Snoqualmie Pass ... 43
The Loop ... 45
Familiar ... 46
Keep This Between Us ... 47
Woven ... 48
I Thought About You All Day While I Worked ... 49
Daytime Moon, Shifts of Season ... 50
The Meaning of Salmon ... 51
Limitations of Guidebooks ... 53
Grieving ... 54

Writing in Light	55
Wind Farms	57
Early	58
Unsent Postcards from Unknown Cities	59
Possessed	60
After the First Seven Days	61
Past Tense, Future Tense	62
Celestial	63
Always Night These Days	64
Blank Days, Black Nights	65
Why We Have Evening	66
Approaching	68
Boundless Desire	69
Completely	71
You Claim I'll Forget You	72
Fill in the Blanks	73
Angels	74
How to Adore	75
Leap Second	76
The Shortest Distance	77
I Just Noticed	78
Fresh Idea	80
How It Is	81
Metamorphosis	82
Translation, 1	83
Translation, 2	83
Dried Fruit on Ben Yehuda Street	84
Dead Sea	85
Winter Drive to Pullman	86
Night Vision	87
Yiddish for Travellers	88
Ritual Baths	90
Scroll	91
Year's End	94
Jamming	95
Rooms	96
Personal Ad	98
Understanding the Rocks	99
Perenniel	106

Clouders

There floating slowly overhead, the Scarlet-Tinged Afflatus,
while to the west a squadron of high-flying Canadian clouds
nudging their way south to the coasts of Mexico to pass the winter,
returning when signaled by the more alert Monarch butterflies.

We lay on our backs on the padded blankets, our thick manual,
The Cloud Watchers' Identification Guide: Pacific Northwest,
ready-to-hand, richly illustrated, the colors and shapes
make us long to spot them, with our binoculars, to record

those vast vaguenesses, the hard-shelled Blue-Gray Bulbous,
leaving its oily vapor-trail, the Snowy Chortler, invisible
but detectable by the gentle sound it makes as it passes (serious clouders
spend hours with cds learning the distinctive low murmurs).

Turning I am fascinated by the clouds in miniature,
sepia-toned, reflected in your sunglasses, I lean as close as I dare
gazing at the beautiful weightless flight, from right lens to left,
of a Narrow-Necked Northwestern Nimbus, we listen breathless

to its barely-audible soprano chugging, like an opera diva
running and singing, and you see the clouds in sepia I see
only in your lenses now reflected back in my pupils, my retinas,
my optic nerves, my brain; that's how close we are.

My Way with Planets

The muscularity of the moon
is nothing to me, it is so many
refreshing cosmic showers
trickling down the spine. Now
Jupiter, say, is another story.
I take advantage of its turgidity,
its obesity, poor peripheral vision.
Come on, you fat planet,
you fubsy orb, with your fussy satellites,
you know, taunting, making it
forget everything wise it has learned
spinning around in the cold, black matter
all these yawning, gaping eons.
Love, your hands warmed my rhomboids,
my obliques, made my trapezius
hard and light as graphite, but
I rely on Jupiter's angry charge
and use its own mass and momentum
against it, rolling the monster
over my shoulders, stepping away nimbly,
with a flick of these two fingers
sending it sailing unstoppably
far beyond Pluto. All this for you,
my love, my succulent pearl;
this is nothing for one of my devotion.

Cyclic

When you apprehend some momentary beauty
your eyes take on such a bright special cast,
I wish you could see them as I see them. By
reflection, refraction, osmosis, I feel your pleasure
in the line of quail rushing across the road (I feel
your worry for them, your hopes for their safety),
in every natural thing I do not notice on my own,
from my tunnel, through my trifocals, my bouncing
monkey mind, always distracted. From where you are,
from where I am, we both looked last night at
the brightest, fullest, closest moon of the year. Urgently
but languidly, oblivious to predators, seventeen-year
cicadas throb and throb and throb, hollow bodies
and tympanum and the seventeen-year wait, clinging
to tree roots and feeding on nothing but the clear fluids,
waiting to find just the perfect mate among the many millions.
They seem so alike to us, these brood-ten cicadas, but
they have their passionate dreams and so filled with hope,
a lesson to me. I sip sap and then emerge and thrum and throb
my hollow body and drum out my song for you so you
can apprehend me suddenly, take me in with those eyes,
let me enter your delicate open ears with my steady
pleading, flowing all over you with my singing.

Nettles

My hands still sport their stigmata: I count
exactly fifty punctures from when I slipped
and fell forward into the nettles, into the
deep, thick, comical tumbleweed, a heap
of brown wigs bristling with hypodermics,
a twenty-foot stack of nested capellini
al dente, rousing, with a woman's name,
Urtica, Urtica Dioica, just arrived at Ellis Island.

But I was so happy until my fall, like Adam,
and I clambered up through the brownery,
squashing through to my knees, in my black
office shoes and pants, not having planned
this expedition. I was so happy to have been
sharing the day with you, so dazzled by you,
the stings were some symbolic reminder
that no one can understand, that no two
people explain the same way, like the goblet
wrapped in a napkin and smashed by the groom's
black shoes, like my shoes. I was as a groom then
when I returned to sit beside you and you
put on your glasses and tried to remove
all the barely visible darts, only discoverable
in silhouette projecting from my dotted palms.
So brave and self-sacrificing. You would
have sucked out the poison if you could,
I would have stretched out on a gurney
and let you perform any surgery, just as you were,
in your youthful pinks and beautiful hair, my skin
flared, and I was so happy, your hands
cooling mine, your smooth, brave cheeks,
your earlobes, your eyes, your lips.

Asking

Would we ever be so used to sharing a bed
we would spend the last half hour
reading our books and saying good night
without making love one more time?
Would we reach the point of watching a film
slouching side by side on a couch
without reaching under each other's clothes,
without throwing everything off,
each ravisher and ravishee, rapturous?
How many thousands of undisturbed nights
would it take, clinging, roiling, roistering,
not to feel that heat, our slick skin,
our delicate organs, soft flowers, sweet
bouquets we keep presenting to each other?

Thin Man in the Bathroom Mirror

Zipping open my fat-man suit and stepping forward,
I lift my feet and step free of it, kick away
that thick pink coating that insulated me,
watching as it sinks into a soft, pink mound.

My body looks so deeply lined now where once
it was bulbous and ballooned, it was a warm Kosher salami,
it was an inflated diving suit, an acorn squash,
now there are those bony ridges and sharp edges.

I wonder that you do not laugh: I laugh myself
(but now I do not jiggle and bobble in delayed waves),
naked I look especially hilarious, I see from the back,
reflected in the mirror, a Javanese demon mask in flesh.

In the bathroom, naked, I whirl like a dervish,
faster and faster to the left and I blush deep pink
as my blood rushes skinward from the centrifugal force,
and the towels blow down, soap falls, from my wind.

I wish you could see the lines of force around me
like a cartoon symbol of speed, like a tornado;
I go so fast the lines spin out from my wrinkles and creases
create dark savage glyphs on the walls and shower door.

I reverse direction and warmed up I go much faster.
I wish you could see me, I wish I could conjure you,
the lines of centripetal force extend across the city
and pull you inexorably back to my spinning heart.

Security

Homeland security can be grasped by
assuming a defensive posture, dropping
in unison and lying on our left sides, my legs
bent under and against your legs, your
right hand reaching around my right hip,
my right arm wrapped around your ribs
right and then left and comforting every
soft smoothness, then the homeland will be
secure for the present. The covers should
be up to our necks, for warmth and privacy,
and there should be enough light so that
I can see the color of your hair just
before my eyes. Once we are secure enough
that way, we shift by an agreed upon signal,
to avoid panic and maintain such well-being,
encoded and decoded and transmitted
through our central nervous systems,
onto our right sides and repeat. As we feel
the security alert change, we turn again
so I am on my back and you are above me
and we whisper the night's secrets, keeping
lips to ears, or breathing in Morse code.
If we fear surveillance, we slide undercover.
Whenever we are out, thanks to these pamphlets,
we can search each other *sub rosa*, quietly
pat each other down, infiltrate, assess and deploy.
We surge against insurgency, check every
thread and layer, every button, every zipper,
every earring, every fold, every hidden place,
safer and calmer, better and better.

Hours and Hours and Hours

In the morning my words
want to remain in the dark.
You must tease them into sound,
wake them with the tip of your tongue,
ring my sonorous uvula, its pealing
booming my words alert.
They jump into the cool air stiff
and with disordered syntax,
dew still filling the centers
of *o*s, *d*s, *b*s, and *p*s
like the truffles in elegant candies.

Hot sun, autumn afternoon.
You are away so I do not see
the sun reflected from your lips.
You are somewhere else so I do not note
the way my idle, concave palm
naturally shapes itself to hold you.
Looking at the leaves, I don't
recall the way your nails so gently
rake my back at the moment
your neck and earlobes suddenly heat.
You are not with me today
so I cannot point out that cake
with chocolate cream
the very color of your nipples.

Aftereffects

Something was different; I don't know.
The radio said it was 107 degrees today,
a record! And I was flushed with pride

to live in such a place, setting records,
rejoicing in the pull of my wet shirt.
At lunch I noticed the wilted lettuce

had such intriguing folds and crenellations,
such complex edging, iridescent doily, wholly
natural, the dressing brightly sweating

beneath the bright lights, each droplet a lamp.
Stuck in traffic, halted by roadwork,
I looked in fresh wonder, even ardor and fervor,

at all the beautiful drivers separately singing,
silently sealed in their cars, the trucks now
hippopotami wallowing, sleekly coated in mud,

or else festooned with their ironically witty
stickers and flags, so endearingly insecure,
their bravado exposed, their drive tribal merely.

Inching along I mouthed to those around me,
"Record high temperature! Not bad!" showing
thumbs up, wanting to celebrate with my community,

to make them enjoy the hidden workings of the body,
of sweat-glands, kidneys, how miraculous.
In my driveway I lay flat in the torrid shadow

to admire the red ants, so energetic, and I took in
with pleasure the persistence of my weeds,
tall and willowy above the heat-stunted grass

and the flowers like ancient parchments ("Not bad!").
When I bit into a cold peach, the touch
of the soft, perfect skin, the tart-sweet juice

welling up around my tongue and palette,
I realized this was all because I was with you today
and everything that followed was transformed.

Reading

You were reading the *Tibetan Book of the Dead* and I was finally asleep. Your lips must have moved as you pronounced the unfamiliar words again and again to make them your own, your tongue pressed against the back of your front teeth, rolling across your palette, the foreign words either overripe with vowels or cacophonous with consonants, but I missed this. My dreams were influenced by the bitter scent of your cigarettes, of the wine in the glass, of the burnt-out sandalwood incense, of the popcorn that was eaten three hours earlier; perhaps it came through to me the sound of the ash you flicked into the bronze lobster ashtray, the sound of the pages turning, of you turning, of the tip of the pencil as it left its marks in your notebook. In my dream you were asleep beside me and I was lying on the propped pillows reading the *I Ching* and I thought about chance and contingency, randomness and the shaping forces of the universe. I struggled to memorize the many almost identical characters saying the Pinyan romanization again and again, my dictionaries weighing down the sheets. In the depth of your sleep you could not know this, but your dreams were shaped by the whispered sounds of Chinese, of the weight of the dictionaries on the sheets, of the squeaky black marker as I tried to draw the characters in my pad, again and again, to memorize the differences. I watched your sleeping face, the way your lips sometimes moved, as if you were saying something again and again. In the depth of your sleep, breathing steadily, your ribs gently expanding and contracting, you dream you were reading the *Tibetan Book of the Dead* and I was finally asleep.

Purity of Essence

In my dream you came to me
wearing a garland of bright,
tubular balloons. What did that mean?
You handed me a glass of water
that was brilliant with sunlight.
"Purity of essence," you said, "like in
Dr. Strangelove." What did you mean by that?
Who else was at that party?
You pointed out Ugo Tognazzi,
Fernando Rey, Toshiro Mifune
(in his samurai gear, his low grunts,
his barking orders, captivating
the cogniscenti). You held my belt
and, flipping it open, you said,
"Better let me adjust this for you."
Your knuckles grazed my stomach
and I asked, "Is this a dream
or what?" "What," you explained,
your red lips fascinating and your eyes
mobile. You pulled me to the dance floor
and when I said I couldn't dance
you popped the buttons of my shirt
one by one, making them whiz past
the other dancers; in the intense heat
of our perfect tango my hands helplessly
slid down your back. You leaped up
so that we were face to face;
your legs locked around my back,
you placed the balloons on my head.
I told you that I love you and you said,
"That must be what this means."

In Your Absence

What a disappointment, the Grand Canyon,
such an enormous hole, going on and on, rocks and dust,
but you were not there.

New faces on the sheets of stamps,
new portraits on the money, all the photos in magazines,
and none of them are yours.

Yo-Yo Ma and Emmanuel Ax exhausted themselves,
Yitzhak Perlman sweated with effort, strings and bows and fingers flew,
but I didn't see you in the concert hall.

Even before my private audience with the Dalai Lama I knew
he'd be pleasant and smile, and speak in his fluty voice,
but he couldn't or wouldn't say where I could find you.

Space exploration, what a waste, planet after planet,
the moon and the stars, comets and asteroids,
it is all a black hole, for you are somewhere on earth.

Papers

I place your page neatly on top of mine,
tapping the edges to line up perfectly,
taking a pleasure in this, our pages on the desk,
lying there together, glowing warmly, edges
aligned, as a spine is aligned, we are aligned,
or as the celestial bodies were in line when we met,
and now there, in the golden pool of light, we lie
text-to-text, like cheek-to-cheek, vis-à-vis,
your fine, slim lines over my bulky ones,
there your minimal, powerful syllables
and there my loose, unshaven sprawl.
How our poems heat up below the desk-lamp.

Thanksgiving

Thankful for you, I prepare a festive meal.
All day I have been gathering what is needed,
Cooking with homage and zeal.

Into the soup I stirred the double cries
of the northern flicker, the raucous love calls
of grosbeaks, plump quail, western tanagers.

I diced some bright dawns to lighten
cloud mushrooms in the salad, nimbus
(say *nimbus* to feel your lips come together).

Mincing some Mingus (*Pithecanthropus Erectus* works well)
I drizzle it over the Persian eggplant
with tomato and yogurt sauce.

Anticipating your smile, your kiss,
I fill ramekins with whole wheat memories,
bake for an hour and melt dreams in a sweet topping.

I cut a thick slice of evening
and serve it fresh and steaming before you
on a dark blue plate with glazed yellow stars.

Psychosomatic

I scan the pear you gave me for your fingerprints,
staring at the yellow skin, glowing like the bulb itself,
until the pear becomes warm and I think of your hand
touching the complex curves, your touch shaping
concavities and convexities, sweetening the pear.
In your absence I swoon, overcome with synaesthesia,
my fingertips hearing the aroma of the yellow, a scent
of desire, I sniff the red grapes and hear their smoothness,
your smoothness, I grow weak, my knees melt, and biting through
the skin of a grape, the spurting juice touching my tongue
produces paroxysms of *outré* images, a dream-vision
of frivolous red-haired seraphim skateboarding into Grand Canyon,
the period that should be at the end of this poem rolling
off the page, across the room, under the bed, glowing all night,
a hot blue-green dot like a whole note in jazz

Tel Aviv

I stand shoulder deep in the hot Mediterranean.
In green-blue fluid I float, my limbs lift,
limbo, akimbo, lumbar, and my black
bathing suit balloons in the water. It is more
amniotic, perhaps, than anything, and I
float and think of you, imagine you with me,
imagine you inside my puffed up black trunks.
The Hebrew word for "jellyfish" is "Medusa,"
but I had no idea when I passed the warning signs.
The beach was crowded yet no one was near me.
I floated in the gentle water feeling your thighs
around my waist, my arms circling you three times,
the motion makes you climb inside my suit
where there's so much room and we press together
and our brains tan as we kiss and float and sweat
even while washed by the waters. Someone shouts,
"Medusa! Medusa!" and we say, "Shalom!"

Sun and Wheatfields

Two Van Goghs I had never seen
made me overjoyed and then strangulated,
heated, excited, but cloistered and caged.
He committed himself to the asylum
and painted the asylum garden, gaudily green,
shiny surfaces, cool shadows, so you want
to feel those thick fronds between thumb
and index finger, thrusting, soothing,
palpable and overwhelmingly healthy, so
happy to be sanctuaried there, so peaceful,
and I thought of you with me in our groves,
our dells and glades, and those painted trees
made me feel cool and happy, smell our Russian olives
as the branches twisted above and around us;
I could hear again the sighing mourning doves.

The second picture was a large drawing,
Sun and Wheat Fields from his asylum window,
just that perspective, all brown toned, pencil,
sepia ink, thousands of wavy lines as the wind
blew through the dry field, the undulations
of the crop bending their tops, the brown sun
all crazed rays of nervous cross-hatchings,
all somehow hot and dusty, unable to escape
the sharp edges and corners of the field, the window,
the paper, the asylum window, the people
just beyond the edge watching Van Gogh,
watching us, keeping all those boundaries
straight, angular, tight, and sharp.

Constrained and edgy, I wanted to find you,
escape with you, you with your curves, with

your lush colors, exotic and earthy, and we'll take
your words, your happy dreams, we'll hide
under those beautiful wavy leaves in the first painting,
leaves thick as elephant ears, thrusting, soothing,
palpable, we'll find asylum just beyond the edges.

Spring Planting

It is the time for preparing the garden again,
time to fix the fence and sprinklers, add compost,
remove all the fall and winter debris.
More aesthetic than practical, I select vegetables
by their physical appearance, by their sexual resonance.

Raking and smoothing the rich soil of the raised bed
my mind soon drifts towards earthy matters.
If I could escape discovery, I would lie down on the bed,
flat on my back, slowly place my arms toe-ward and then
drag them in bold curves through the fertile ground.

Then jumping off, I'd sneak away and watch
as later you would find the imprinted dirt archangel.
I will have you in mind when I plant the tomatoes
with their soft, smooth skin, their blushing color,
their compelling and lingering taste, their modesty.

How blatant should I make my raised bed, since
even young people, walking by on the sidewalk,
might see through the many holes and gaps in the cedar fence
yellow-neck squash flirting with the Brussels sprouts,
Japanese eggplant, thick fingers intertwined with vines?

Yoga Practice

I keep trying to practice yoga,
but I can't follow the directions.
I can't send my spine skyward
or sink my sitting bones into the earth.
Only you could make me extend
such distances, rise and sink
simultaneously, and only you
know just where my sitting bones are.
I am so distracted by the lovely words
Adho Mukha Svanasana, Dandasana,
and I chew the syllables, tossing them
in my mouth left to right like jujubes,
danda danda dandasana and I fail
to check that my pelvic rim is parallel to the floor
(I need your hands to find my pelvic rim, to see
my thighbones are grounded, *feefifofum*,
ramalamadandasana), that my spine is lengthened.
I can't even breathe properly; each inhale,
each exhale, a word like exile, should be all.
I am instructed to count, to think
only inhale, only exhale, but my thoughts
sink and rise and search you out,
what do you look like when you do this,
or *sitting forward bend* (my, but you bend
so beautifully, I want to wrap myself
around you and bend with you, inhale
with you, exhale with you, like so)
Paschimottanasana, feeling the heat of you
really helps me concentrate, my back
rolls and melts and can flow both
skyward and earthward, my pelvic rim
is clear to me now, syllables sweet

and sticky, my lying-draped-around-you bones
are in especially good order and my breath
seeps uncounted and audible exactly
in rhythm with yours.

Japanese Style

When I see Japanese homes
with their taut, rice-paper walls,
sunlight flooding in on polished wood,
tatami mats, screens, fans, scrolls,
I think how pleasing it would be
to live in such a place, natural,
organic, aesthetic, somehow purer,
uncluttered, focused, whole.

But if I moved into such a place,
I know I could not sleep except fitfully,
rolling from side to side across the floor,
my head throbbing on the wooden pillow.
I would wake from a dream of you
and spend my nights covering the paper walls
with my wild, illegible writing, describing you,
making imaginary letters, long apologies,
poems, graffiti, questions, confessions,
my kimono creased and wrinkled,
spotted with pencil, ink stains, and sweat,
and I'd be unable to stop until
I had filled all of the walls of the house
with words for you, floor to ceiling,
room after room, each slowly dimming
as the sunlight was blocked.

Snow Flocking, Signs of Solstice

Cold fog inside the glass, and beyond
birds heading in no particular direction,
sometimes circling, not feeding, not migrating,
not mating, not nesting, but just flying
in sheer joy, their chevrons and triangles
black on the sizing of the winter sky.
We stand outside to read their signs but
then we are not reading, not watching,
not feeding, heading in no particular direction,
your skin so hot beneath all those layers,
the light on your hair and in your eyes.
Electromagnetic waves and strands of static,
your hair fluttering as the wind picks up,
the birds en masse with a downward tremble
of wings, the bare boughs creaky in the cold,
and I catch your earring and your wave
as the clouds open and you are silently assumed,
and it is dark already, it is the shortest day.

Permeable

In my dream I was the ocean
surging and lapping an irresistible beach.
You came and swam in me every day,
and even with my millions of miles
I felt your plunge, your first steps,
your softest soles and tentative toes.
My foamy waters warmed as they climbed
your legs, your stomach, and my waves
crested and tried to attract your gaze.
You gave yourself to my salty waters.
Your tongue tasted me, I tasted you,
and filled the small valleys between your ribs,
the tinier ridges of your fingerprints,
my drops on your face, your brave
immersion in me total. I buoy you
(you girl me, a joke little oceans tell).
Afterwards, still an ocean, I dream
I am the clear, pure water spraying
steamily out of a bright chrome faucet,
washing the salt and sand from you,
foamy now with soap, slippery, laving,
entering you everywhere, loving,
zesty, hot, yet like the ocean.

Family History

My people hail from Machu Picchu and Vladivostok
and my great-grandmother was half coyote.
She was famous for howling at the moon
in the backyard, well into her eighties.

Uncle Zheng, baffled and battered by political swings,
was in the end fired from his job at the sperm bank.
It's so hard to take up a new career, one-legged,
given to visions, and three feet and half feet at the shoulder.

Every fall when the geese formed their great Vs
Mother sneaked down to the docks and ran off to sea.
A congenital condition, salmon or sea turtle genes,
while Father found consolation with yoga and tai chi.

She returned in May in her worn yellow slickers,
reeking of fish, showing off her tattoos and scars.
Please don't ask about my sister with her Hopi husband,
and about my aunt's coven, my lips are sealed.

It's true I haven't been all I should have been
and my relatives are embarrassed when they see me.
But you, with your big toe stuck in the bathtub faucet,
shouldn't laugh at me at all, you shouldn't laugh at all.

Tales of the Cruise

My aunt comes back from the cruise
with tales of adventure.
The food, the music, the exotic customs,
all the amateur anthropology
of the eighty-year old widow.
A single figure stands apart in her narrative,
a salesman, retired, also eighty.
"He was so persistent," says my aunt coyly,
"he prepositioned me all the way to Venezuela."

I picture the scene clearly. At the dinner table
he leaned across the salad plate
and said to my aunt with a wink, *"With. Amid. Between."*
And dancing one of their slow, shuffling fox trots,
one of their slow, shuffling tangos,
his thin lips whispered to her earring, *"Of. Unto. Despite."*
My aunt backed away from his arms.
"Please," she whispered hoarsely, urgently,
"I must think of my poor Nat, may he rest in peace."
She sits down at the table and takes a pill.
The salesman tried to restrain himself
through the costume party, the Casino Night,
through the Gaucho Bar-B-Q, and the comedians.
When they are by the shuffleboard court
(everyone slathered in sunblocker, wearing dark glasses),
in seductive tones he chants to her alone,
"About. At. For. Within."
My aunt is refined and cautious.
She looks towards the green islands and responds,
"Past. But. Except. Over."
And they speak of their greatgrandchildren
and they ride the pink jeeps.

Poem for Lunch

The poem you sent me today for lunch
was so satisfying; it kept me nourished all day.
The words were low in fat but high in protein,
your descriptions were pungent, especially
where you speak of us meeting, and we both enjoy
those fleshy double-entendres, the fortified metaphors,
soy similes that can take on the flavor of the sauce.
I was thrilled by your light handling, by your breath,
warm soufflé, a puff crossing the surface of hidden skin.
The poem you sent me today for lunch
was so natural, rich in Omega-3 fatty acids and alliteration,
it lowered my cholesterol and raised key parts of my body,
the way you described the meeting of your croissant,
with its soft, smooth, buttery curve, a smile, a moon,
and my veggie-sub; it made me picture you
today at your yoga class, the hot room,
your black leggings, your spaghetti straps.

These Are My Crustacean Days

All I can do is attach myself
to the rocky bottom and wait.
I will be a decorator crab (come,
my love, dance with me the old
Cyclocoeloma tuberculata, dip and twirl,
let me raise up and encircle your back).
With my clumsy claws I festoon
my hard shell with whatever catches you.
No anemones or coral polyps, but
the sound of an owl flying nearby,
a wonderful poem, that interview on NPR,
sculptures made of icicles and twigs,
all fixed to my exoskeleton.
How grand and charismatic I must be!
I watch and wait for you, green eyes
at the end of my eyestalks, scanning.
I dig up some sand from the ocean bottom,
chew and polish and work it with my
crab lips and crab teeth, my loving crab tongue,
and when you kiss me again one day
I will pass to you the most perfect,
smooth, opalescent pearl.

Monet's *The Magpie*

Has the magpie just landed or is it
about to fly off? Is it morning or late afternoon?
Monet doesn't say, so I have decided
it is a male bird of the most intense devotion.
He has been waiting since noon for his
beautiful partner, waiting for her
to land there beside him on the skewed fence,
attuned to the sound of her soft feathers.
Snow upon snow, he searches
for the familiar, nimble Ys of her small feet.
He found some treasures he saved to give her,
a sweet wedge of tangerine, a quarter
of a whole wheat bagel, that was hard to carry,
even though he is large for a magpie. He looks
north, the sun behind him, trying to give
the best appearance for when she flies up.
While he waited he made up a new tune
he wants to sing to her, hoping his love will be
obvious and will heat her beneath her fine plumage.

Snoqualmie Pass

There was that moment when the tires seemed
no longer in contact with anything, when the slide
at that slow speed, like those Sergio Leone Westerns,
that slow pulling out of guns from holsters, the slow
close up of the sweat falling down the craggy face,
the bright splash of blood, snail's pace charge,
the dead villain floating backward off the horse
disappearing in the dust, then all returns to normal speed.
The moment I looked at you as the car slowly slid
first left then diagonally across the right lanes, Yeats'
gyre came to mind, widening spire, no footing,
no mooring, no traction, but there was this crazy
beauty in the snow blowing horizontally out of the woods,
fat snowflakes like winter owls lit by headlights from trucks,
the only lights coming in slivers through the fence
separating northbound from southbound, and who
wrote "Snowbound"? I wondered, and you were
so lovely in the light from the snow and the trucks,
I wasn't worried, the car in its skidding over the ice.
It had its loveliness, like skaters only more graceful
and without the annoying music, your eyes wide and
intently interested in it all, that complete attention,
our breathing stopped while watching it happen,
our car somehow sliding completely around, coming
to a gentle, silent stop, inches from the railing,
perfectly lined up, you said afterward, as if I had
parallel parked, but our lights facing the way we had come.
Then we both breathed, and then continued, ice and snow
bright and cheerful, rushing at the windshield, and it
was as if the film had resumed normal speed. That night
from our window we watched the snow falling into the fields;
in the snug room I felt that floating slow motion slide

that freedom from earth, from traction, from gravity, the light coming in through slivers where the curtain did not close completely, and the one light we left on, your eyes shot me through the heart, your skin lit me with celebratory flames, and we slid breathless, weightless, fused, floating without gravity.

The Loop

You think I have a one-track mind, but actually
I entertain several notions at once. For instance,
if I am thinking how odd it is that national anthems
(*Star-Spangled Banner, O Canada*, let alone the more stirring
Chee-lai! Boo yuan tzo noo lee dee run men
or the more rhythmic *Ragupati ragava rajah Rum*)
can only be handled by massive choral groups,
by opera divas and gospel singers, and can't be played
by amateurs on guitar, and isn't that counter to
national purposes? I could think along these lines
for minutes without recalling even once how
when you finish exercise your skin shines
and you glow with inner heat. Or just last night
I spent several minutes watching the news
(*Pipebombs in Rural Mailboxes, Rolling Stones Launch World Tour*),
before phrases from your note came to me ("a serious kiss,"
"hand sliding beneath the sheet," "do you like garlic?")
and I lost my ability to concentrate and thought of you again.

Familiar

Gabbles of geese,
raw-voiced blackbirds,
cut winter fog,
cool and recumbent,
slumbering in the field.

I hear their foreign phrases
before their milling
gray black figures emerge
emerge from the mist, davening,
a minyan dutifully
gathering to say Kaddish.

Keep This Between Us

Once I didn't hear any water running,
any sounds of showering, of teeth being brushed,
of flushing, but the light glowed
under the bathroom door while I waited
in the dark bedroom in the crumpled sheets.
Your feet made shadows and sometimes
I heard soft noises like *aaucch!* and *ooeocch!*
I pushed the door open and you wheeled
startled as if you had forgotten I was waiting,
and naked before the glaring mirror
you had powdered your face, made your lips,
your eyelids, your cheeks all light blue.
For some reason you had an impulse
to see what you would look like dead,
to imagine your parents having to identify you,
and you made the noises while sticking your tongue
as far as possible first to the left and then to the right,
trying to find your best side. To show me
you stuck out your tongue and said *aaucch!* and *ooeocch!*
Your body was cold and I kissed your blue lips
mourning my loss, feeling the absence,
your tongue stiff against mine.

Woven

When we finally pull back from each other,
steamy and besotted, still breathing in unison,
some of my hairs stick to you, small, curled, straight,
gray and black writing, almost letters.
As I pick them from you I see they are
mainly *I*s and *C*s and *U*s. It is a message
written by our bodies, my body to your body,
I C U perhaps, or when I hug you tightly
against me once more, *I seize you*.
I always remove this detritus from your
smooth, clear skin, this warm, creamy paper
for my aboriginal rebuses. *U* and *I*.
Now I think you should have kept all that hair
rubbed off in the friction and passion,
you should have filled bags with it,
had it spun into wool and knitted to form
a beautiful warm, magical sweater,
thick, mottled gray and black, to hug you
tightly, snug protection against the elements.
When you sit to write on a dark, rainy day,
you could rub your hand across the sweater,
over your breasts and stomach, feeling
the snap of static electricity, and you'll think
of how we make each other's nerves spark.

I Thought About You All Day While I Worked

Last night the two stars I could see were umlauts
over an invisible pursed o, an *ö*. By dawn
the last yellow and white leaves hanging frailly from
my paper birch were dried cedillas and *ñ*s,
the frosted grass so many accents and quotation marks.

I thought about you as I sat up in bed and stretched,
going from hyphen to circumflex to accent grave.
You filled my mind as I pulled on my work-clothes,
my bones snapping, my fingers readying themselves,
one light in my room brighter than the gray dawn moon.

I plunged into work, deeply, and through the brightening day
trudged and dragged and pushed along, thinking of you,
carelessly tossing my sweater aside as I grew rosy with the work,
traversing the broad white plane again and again, digging holes
in parallel lines and dropping my words in, smoothing the surface.

Tonight I collapse in the bed again, thinking of you,
my sore body, bent for hours close to the glowing white field,
relaxes into a comma or a single parenthesis. I think
ahead towards the harvest when I hope all my seed-words
please you in the Spring by their perfume and eye-delighting colors.

Daytime Moon, Shifts of Season

Geese impress their triangular cuneiform
across the broad white tablet of the river;
the fluttering wind of their broad wings
stir the crisp text into illegible blurs.

You defined the landscape; it emulated
the gray triangles within the green of your eyes;
it reached after that green, and the leaves shook
with passion, tinged with the red of your toenails.

The trees erupting into autumn took on the shaggy,
soft brown of your sweater, summer's flowers
toned down into the subdued and stylized blooms
on your warm socks, showing through your sandals.

What is your reading of the twigs today? The broad
leaves of the mimosa, the fallen, serrated orange
plant debris dropping with a sound of rain upon us
write their cryptic marginalia on the black blanket.

The Meaning of Salmon

Twelve years in the Pacific Northwest I now understand
the underlying meaning of salmon, the mental hold
salmon maintains on people who are living here.
If asked, if they are at public hearings or budget meetings,
they speak of the economic importance of salmon,
elsewhere, the tradition of salmon for native culture,
or the environmental impact, as endangered species.
But none of those capture the symbolic meaning
that remains constantly and swiftly moving in an
undercurrent of thought, a stream of consciousness.
People here attach themselves to salmon because
of the great spawning journeys they undertake, from
ocean to rivers and streams, against the flow,
up waterfalls, over dams, past the outcast nets,
and people see this as romantic, though they won't
bring such a thing to consciousness, the salmon
going through all that, lunging upstream, up fish ladders,
are like lovers, are seeking the fulfillment of desire,
they are so crazed by love they will not turn back
when it's more logical and rational to do so, when
they could loaf around until they die of old age
in some nice deep, calm section of the ocean,
or some beautiful, sunspeckled pool below a waterfall.
The people of the region watch the salmon runs
because they identify with the salmon, with their
love-melancholy and sexual drive, so that a sort
of erotic perfume must fill the air over these states.
It was not clear to me until I began thinking about you
recently, and people were discussing the salmon quest.
Now when I walk near the Columbia and see
the rippled water flowing, I wonder if those
breaks in the surface are salmon, and my mind drifts,

I think about things you have said. I picture finding
a salmon one day snagged in a bit of line or some plastic wrap,
or maybe swimming up to me one Rosh Hashanah when
I go down to cast out bread and say *tashlich*. And this
special salmon can speak, and it says, "Since you
understand the meaning of salmon, I will grant you
anything you wish." I spend the next two hours
telling this salmon about you, about my desire, about
romance, then I give it some bread for its journey
and send it on its way over the dams, up the waterfalls,
and nightly I await the happy outcome to my wish.

Limitations of Guidebooks

I noticed, after we have been together,
a bird appears. If we are lying down,
I might see it hover like a frothy moth
up at the top of the tree canopy,
its curly, round body and isosceles wings
silhouetted so I can see discern it although
my glasses are way over there, folded up,
inside my shoe. I can see its pink beak,
and when it spreads its wings it is like
a circus tent or auto-sale awning, alternating
stripes of gray and red; it makes its nest
from shredded silver excelsior, catching
the light of either sun or moon. I realized
that while we were dancing our a capella tango,
al fresco, a la mode, a summerheat dance,
a family of quailish Quetzacoatls bobbed by,
their rainbow plumage gaudy and iridescent,
as any of their kind, as any birds brought forth
ex nihilo by passionate rush together,
not noted in Audubon, Sibley or Peterson.

Grieving

I have seen you gaining the confidence of the large ruffled dog,
the one with scratches and scars, the one panting in the small
dim shadow of sagebrush, and you pet it, you look for a collar,
you bring it in your truck and take it cool water and food
from a Mexican restaurant, and this is one dog of many.
So I knew you would understand that when my sheltie died,
my first dog though I am so ancient, I knew you would not laugh
to know I recited the mourner's Kaddish, though he wasn't
strictly speaking Jewish; still he loved challah and leaped
ecstatically every time he heard the blessing over the bread.

Writing in Light

I have only five photographs of you,
all taken by strangers over the last year.
They can be arranged in a story:
there you are alone, in a net hammock,
a metaphor of suspense and entanglement,
of being above the earth, and yet below
the Heavenly Halls, my angel, my sweet,
so subtly posed, your plumage out of the frame.

There we are in the official group photo,
you barely brought into the picture, shy,
youthful, such cheeks, those legs and arms,
the man who had his arm around your shoulder
happy to this day, so lucky to be near you.
Where am I? O, back, way back, as always,
mine is the barely legible face a foot above the others,
you can't see my eyes, but they are looking towards you,
you can't see my brain or my heart, they are filled with you.
We are separated by only twelve festive people, their plaids,
their sunhats, their faces silently saying *Cheese*, but
we are at least in the same frame, together.

Then these last three pictures, over-exposed, taken
by strangers in parking lots, by coffee places, using
a cheap, disposable camera, are surprisingly the best.
We are in the brightest light, we outshine everything,
my arm around you, your bare arm, your waist,
your arms around me, we are together, we are alone,
finally, we are lit with happiness, we are blessed,
we are purified, we are holy, we are the sun and moon,
so gladdened we transcend the spectrum, we are
absolutely complete, rejoined, reformed, one,

the mountains and cars, the shop signs and windows,
they are illusions, we are all, we are written in light.

Wind Farms

Let us run off faraway, to the west, to one of those
dry unloved ridges, beyond the army training area,
beyond the Indian reservation with its casinos, land
scorched or sagebrushed, where the winds tickle
the fat rocky toes of the foothills of the Cascades.
No one will look for us there; we can be wind farmers.

It will take hard work with such unpromising soil
but in a few years think of the pleasures of our land.
There will be the acres of chinooks and harmattans
blowing off hats, rocking trailers passing on the interstates.
Zephyrs and mistrals will hang like pupae from the mulberries,
when ripe cracking open to blow hotly at harvest time.

Our handcrafted simooms will snap across the tables
at the farmer's markets, trade winds we use for swapping
(we'll take boxes of Santa Anas and frilly fresh Föhn
for steamy sirocco or refreshing sea-breezes, tailwinds,
baby cyclones, though we refuse to take the doldrums).
At the county fair we judge kids' squalls and eat soufflés.

Boundary layer winds will ruffle your silky hair, while
my wind farmer's nose will sense shifts in the coriolis force.
My hands feel your pressure gradient from high to low,
our skin responds to the sun's supersonic winds. We'll toss off
pants and windsocks with the gusts and gales, each breeze.
Aeolian harps hum, while winded we breathe and sigh.

Early

I watch for you and breathe in
thick winter fog, breathe out
steamy aromatic memories
I had inhaled when last with you.
I balance the breaths, juggle
the frosty earth and whitened plants,
the pale smudge in the sky that is the sun,
the paler smear that is the moon,
the icy malingering mud,
the dark matter between celestial bodies,
all on the one hand, while on the other,
your earlobe held by my lips, your
suddenly hot cheek, your tropical sigh.
I stare at the horizon, my eyes fixed for you,
and I am already with you, I am open.
Starlings and juncos mistake the fog
frozen on my eyes for infinite sky.
Turning, wheeling, squawking
squadrons of black birds enter my open eyes
and fill my entire body with their wild cries.
They exult and sing and their flapping wings
tickle and heat me as I stand waiting,
watching for you to arrive
with your beauty and sweet hot breath.

Unsent Postcards from Unknown Cities

Bleak and drizzly day but walked for hours. At night
my toes curled from the cold. Pretended you were asleep beside me.
I whispered for hours everything I wanted to say to you.
Wish you would hear.

Spent two hours in a café happy I could not understand
anything anyone said. Pretended to read newspaper
written in runes and rebuses. Didn't relax until I felt my
hand take the shape of you, my thumb resting inside your pelvis.
Hope you are well.

Sweltering hot and the sweat pours from me. Remember
how wonderful it was when we exchanged fluids?
Miss you wildly night and day.

Lingered in the old part of the city until I felt like a dusty,
crumbling ruin myself. Sat outside in the rain afterward,
eroding, oxidizing, developing a soft patina.
How are things there?

Crumpled on this hotel carpet, I dream your hands
twist me into Half-Lord-of-the-Fishes Pose. I turn
and fall gracefully open, unscrewed at the hips. Stroke
my inner threads.
Have you been sleeping well?

Tonight there is no sign of the moon; you must have it
with you. Climb inside it and hover above your lover.
Forgive my lunacy. XOXO

Possessed

At this time of night what are you doing?
Maybe you are in bed, reading, under blankets,
glowing in a yellow pool of incandescence.

You have your glasses on, the brown retro frames,
your hair is smoothed back, and you are wearing
a smooth, soft white nightgown, maybe a smile.

I remember every time we were ever together.
Now, far away from you, I envy things.
That's how low I go, so removed from bliss.

I envy first your nightgown, wishing that I
could be wrapped around you in contact with your skin.
I would be wool and flannel, your silk long johns.

I envy the sheets and mattress that get to sustain you
every night, raising you to that pure place of your dreams.
Your dreams soak through me, sweeten me.

I envy the book you hold open on your bent legs,
because you are holding it with both hands,
because your eyes are focused on it, its pages

just below your breasts, sometimes touching,
and you are getting pleasure from its words. Yes,
to be your focus, to give you pleasure, I envy that.

After the First Seven Days

The phone never rings but that's no surprise. The
cell-phone is a gray ornamental statue, a useless
totem I carry. There are no new voicemails,
but you told me you couldn't call. Always *O
unread messages* in my e-mail, but you said
you shouldn't write. Food looks delicious
but it's tasteless and always too much for one.
What's the point of coffee now? My restless legs
kickstart me at night and I rumble out unable to stop.
I look for you and wonder if you look for me,
if you feel hollowed out and shredded, as I do.
All week my back hurt from sitting shiva on a low stool.

Past Tense, Future Tense

My naïve calendar has so much sadness now
I could not stand it. Little did I know,
little did I know. I snipped away the foul days.
I completely excised whatever was that
month after February, its name I will not mention.
If it comes up accidentally, I drown it out
with whirling greigers and stamping feet. April
turned out far better, though individual days
when we could not be together, these I carefully
snipped away, performing daychotomies,
weekectomies, and sutured the ragged sad edges
together, wetting the wounds as needed
with my abundant fluids, all my excess. I expanded
those few times we were together, those dates
receiving hour-augmentations; I botoxed my tongue,
the tips of my fingers, to seal inside me those
recollections of you, the spectacular aerie,
the tiny bits of time, ticking, always ticking.
May and the first days of June, little did I know,
little did I know, so wonderful and blissful,
joyful in my last days, my running out of sand,
and now these blanks of time, soggy, unprinted
months with no days, no light, no passionate glowing.

Celestial

Clearly the entire purpose of the sun
is to illuminate you, to shine upon you,
and from this process the sun
obtains vitamin D which can then
be distributed to people elsewhere,
the sun basks in your smile, it glows
by reflecting you, it obtains its heat
from your heat, and when you lie down,
your royal purple silks in a small
pile beside the bed, this is what we call
the *zenith* of the sun, and when you go,
this is the *nadir*, the sad, cold dark.

Always Night These Days

A weeklong eclipse; so dark these days.
I can't see your back when I draw your shadow.
Today you didn't fling your clothes off
and I am in a cold coal mine this dank June.

My heart leaks powdered graphite
across gray cold-pressed paper, with tooth.
My bituminous hands and anthracite eyes
paint you as I stare where the sun once was.

Blank Days, Black Nights

In the dark my clenched eyelids
are fringed with wild blue paisleys
and it's sad you can't see them.

Today perhaps you wore a retro-
tie-dyed shirt, faux leopard-skin bra,
those long earrings I almost swallowed.

It's terrible I did not see you. My throat
is filled with dust these days and if I sing
a gray puff of ash floats from my mouth.

When you last wrote you said you were *tipsy*.
Sweet love, you can't peel me from you:
I am your skin. I am tipsy with you.

Why We Have Evening

Three days in a row we clung
so tightly together, our surfaces
and depths were permeated,
our hollows and gaps filled. Then
you were inside my auricles,
I lounged in your ventricles,
you inhaled and I exhaled,
one breath, one beat. I have you
now in my lungs, you hold me
right there, and there, even there.
You perform miracles and file
my toadish flesh smooth, you
turn me into hot oil and I
pour into you forever. Such a time.
On the drive back the deep blue
shadows fall across the freeway
and we talk about the way dark saddens.
But now that you carry me inside
your bones, your cute pink colon,
your little big toe, under your tongue,
inside your breasts, every place I
have adored and pressed, you have
new strength and joy. Take a really deep breath
and feel me inside you again. *Ahhhhh*.
This part of the day is to soothe
and calm, to wring out any unpleasant thoughts
to strain out the nightmares through the
holes in the black and blue sky.

That is why each night we have evening.
Unhappy extremes of day or night are wiped
clean; they cascade down from our bodies

and swirl around below our interlocked feet.
You become happy and light and purified
again every evening as again and again,
we rejoin each other, back to steady joy,
flowing over us in a hot, foamy stream.

Approaching

Now I understand the double-meaning of *rush*
when I am approaching you, especially, as today,
after a lonesome gap of days and distance,
approaching you through time and space.
If there were hooligans in our town,
if there were Cossacks or Visigoths waiting
at the next red light, trying to keep me from you,
I could evade them, leave them howling,
for I have strength and speed when approaching you;
if there were famished packs of wolves or even
clouds of mosquitoes and gnats, if my car were mired
in traffic or in mud to the door handles,
I would keep approaching you, surround you
fuzzily, like iron filing around a strong magnet;
if I couldn't find any of my shoes, if I misplaced my glasses,
I would wrap towels around my feet, I'd tap my way
with a branch from my paper birch tree,
across the Cascades, across the Horse Heaven Hills,
down Rattlesnake Flats, I wouldn't be stopped.
I could find you by just recalling how you looked
the last time I saw you, how you felt and tasted,
your voice remembered, I rush and rush.

Boundless Desire

Another empty day but I had
the constant sense you were nearby.
I was so certain, I put on my shoes
and hiked the neighborhood,
as if you could be waiting, watching,
suppressing your glee. I prayed
you would jump down as I passed
underneath your limb. You are
my phantom limb. Once you told me
there are eleven dimensions and
slightly or very different events
are taking place simultaneously
in parallel universes. At this moment
in some dimension, you are wearing
a tight black tuxedo jacket, smooth
black tights and a top hat. In that universe
I am your lovely assistant, my sequins
dazzling the audience, my gold jacket,
gold teeth, massive earrings and
fluorescent green-blue peacock feathers.
You place me in the isolation booth,
close me in so just my eyes are visible,
as you slide the heavy red and black
panels with the gold calligraphy
we copied from the menu of our
favorite Thai restaurant. You have
the most exciting act in this dimension.
I try to signal impossible commands
with my eyes, all that's left of me.
Let the magician disappear as well,
with her lovely assistant. The audience will cope.
You slide the last panel in (on the other side

are the characters for Phad Euwe with tofu)
and the trapdoor slides open sending me
here to this universe and I am waiting,
waiting, waiting, waiting for you
to drop here beside me. I will clothe you
in my sequins and faux feathers.

Completely

I love you alphabetically and algebraically,
my cosine adjacent to your hypotenuse.
I love you boldly and beatifically,
I love you constantly and comprehensively.
I love you devotedly; daily you dizzy me.
I love you with excessive exuberance,
I love you with fervor and fondness
(I find you are such fun, we fondle frequently).
I love you gently and gratefully,
I love you heroically; you heap happiness upon my head.
I love you with intensity, I love your eyes.
I love you January or June, I just love you.
I love you on and on and on through all,
I love you in Zen with zeal and zest,
I play my zither and sing a wild zouk,
a soulful zemirah, a heated Zydeco,
then begin loving you starting again with A.

You Claim I'll Forget You

When my brain and body
fade and fail and fall away,
you will be in my mind
like a glowing ember, giving
my soul a quick flurry of kisses
as it leaves me, maybe sparking
me once more to life, like
a jump given to a dead battery.
You will give a quick caress, a
friendly squeeze to my dried-out parts.
When I can't tell flan from flannel,
I will rejoice in recalling you;
when my lobes are free of clutter
(favorite foreign fragments,
Zweckmassigkeit ohne Zweck,
Ma nishtanah ha-leila hazeh,
all those novels and poems,
street names, my name),
I will remember perfectly
how you looked in that black
nightgown our very first night
in a room, the champagne
we could not uncork, or
that once we opened ourselves
we could not be bottled up
ever again.

Fill in the Blanks

You never gave me the personality inventory test.
I would be willing to take it, naked with you
draped gracefully bare over my fuzzy form.
You could hold your clipboard out, while
I would lick you there and there (even there).
Now it would be handy if I had such an inventory
to find out what is left of my personality.
In that battered cardboard box with all the masking tape
you find round red stacks of passion and desire
dried like red lentils. Hidden behind a false wall
you find my pickled hope while I kiss beneath your arms,
the back of your thighs. Let me hold you up
while you search the highest shelves for my love,
my happiness. Call out whenever you find
something, write it down on the chart, add the scores.

Angels

All the angels in paintings and films
are so far off the mark it astonishes.
Research shows angels are plump,
tentacled, glossy black and neon orange,
splotched with iridescent bronze.
They have the husky voices of actresses
Angelica Houston and Angelina Jolie.
They never stop moving (some say
they can't stop or they will sink to the sidewalk),
their bulbous black eyes always wide open,
always moist, their lips pouty and pursed.
Their skin is so thin you would be able to see
their internal organs if angels were as large
as mosquitoes. They hover near ears
and hiss and sing, insist and cajole until
you brush the whole cloud of them away.
The tips of their fins whine as they hover,
their black tentacles tickle my lobes.
Flights of angels speed up my auditory canal
whispering about how wonderful you are,
reminding me of what you said or how you looked,
filling me with thoughts of you when we are apart.
Some angels wait by my eyes until a drop
rolls hot and fresh from a tear duct. They
cradle the drop with their tentacles
then they all rush away to feed.

How to Adore

I realize after seeing you I need a new language
since standard speech is tarnished, mundane,
mangled and mingled. I need to say,
kummy huouma nippradaybee and let us
loobamisty fagwa woly. Today you were so
m'dnotu psoochy, if I can be so bold,
you dizzied me with your *guofhan so*,
and the way you *zdooble-ha-kata*. No one
has ever *zdoobled* as you *zdooble*.

I know I need to purify myself before we meet.
I need to take three showers beginning at dawn
and recite my psalms to you while I drip-dry
naked in the bright new sun. Psalm 688,
in particular, should be part of the daily liturgy,
since it is splashed over with your beauty,
my manuscripts blurry from hot water,
herbal soaps, as I sing in praise of your *tebnosh*,
your perfect *ulla-rosh fimmla*, your sweet
afnokoos I love to kiss. After chanting,
I dress in hand-painted silks, dazzling colors,
thin so they don't restrict my dances to you,
the *cha-cha-freilich* and the twirling dance
as yet unnamed where for at least three minutes
I stay ten inches above the floor.

Leap Second

The news of the leap second excited me;
I was only concerned with misspending it,
a lost youth, a dissipated middle-age.
You could have been standing naked on my back
squeezing the melancholy from my chakras,
your toes curling gently while I exfoliated.
They said physicists measure a second by
the excited waggling of Cesium 133,
though its passionate vibrations could
not be greater than mine. In the leap second
my blood would have gushed gaily
through several feet of arteries feverish for you,
scarlet for you, I could have drawn in
a deep breath of you or noticed how
the soft ridges of our fingerprints fit together.
We could have leaped as one in the leap second,
hands interlocked, our four feet for that moment
two feet above the crushed bedsprings,
flying heavenward. I could have opened my eyes
from deepest sleep in the leap second
to see your face beside mine, to forget the world,
to forget everything else except you.

The Shortest Distance

I paint a sepia line, freehand,
my smallest brush, a barely
perceptible dot of water,
so the line's edges shade into
a wash, the wash a shadow.
I lean down until my nose
almost touches the wet line,
the puckered paper, my back
curved, and I stare until
the line becomes you, my
memory adding your body
around the line, your geometry,
your curves, your volume,
your shapes and shadows,
your colors and softness,
your heat and sweet scents.

I Just Noticed

My mouth is unraveling. You must
have taken my lips away with you
when we were last together. They
paired so well with yours, our four lips
so mobile and attached to each other.
Yes, now, remember you held my
lower lip with your teeth, so gently
it didn't hurt at all, when you pulled it
out to you, and I was so happy
with all that we were doing, I didn't
notice it was missing until days later.
The upper lip, I just now remember
your tongue rolling across its length
below the line of moustache in
the rain-shadow of my mighty nose.
That must be when it also went with you.
What could I notice after your note?
You said you couldn't see me and
I couldn't see. The entire week was pitch black
I thought because my face was pressed
deep into my carpet. When I finally
felt my way to the bathroom mirror
and flipped the light switch I thought of
power outage, nuclear war, earthquake.
What difference does any of that
matter to me, without you? I felt
pleased by the blackness because I could use
the cataclysm to find you. In the chaos
we could be rejoined. But then I realized
you had pocketed my eyes that last day
(*we couldn't see each other*! such a punster!)
Please keep them until we meet again;

my eyes are happiest when they are on you.
Leave them out as much as possible
wherever you are, whatever you are doing,
and they will be refreshed, the whites
will be whiter and the darks moist and
the ducts ready to flow. My eye-hollows
don't matter. Whatever else of me you have
keep with you wherever you might be,
day or night, I don't need any of me,
and I'll try to keep from unraveling
more than absolutely necessary.

Fresh Idea

Unable to do anything about my brain,
I make what repairs I can to my body.
Two hours at the dentist getting filled,
filled with X-rays and numbing fluids
that get no further than my mouth
when my pain is deeper and elsewhere.
I flap my bitewings and nod when they show me
the unreal specters of my alleged teeth.

I get my hair and beard cut short and
in the mirror see Vincent Van Gogh
from one of the late self-portraits, if my
hairs were each orange and an eighth-inch thick
and if the towel was a bandage around the side
of my head. If I sent you my ear, I know
you'd recognize it without a note. You'd
unwrap it when you were finally alone,

spread wide open in the middle of your pillow
where it was slightly depressed from your
beautiful head, my ear fits perfectly and feels
tingly from your familiar fingers. You could
unwrap it every day and tell it everything,
fill it with all you would like to say, drop
hot tears into the center, breathe into it,
trace all its folds and crenellations.

After a week, when it is completely filled,
a plump pink ear scone, you can smuggle it
back somehow and I can wear it once more,
listening to your murmurs and laughs again and again.

How It Is

The cells of the big, dry brushes swell
when they are dipped into the cool
tower of water in the thick coruscated jar,
my hand rubbing the fossil ribs. Swelling
bristles soften as they quickly thicken
and I tap the wood against the open
lips of the jar to splash off the extra,
always far more water than can be absorbed
by all of the jars of dry brushes put together.
I think of you, I think of us, in every
act and image of my day and night.
My cells fill with you wholly, holy,
and the brushes take in such colors
to spread across the skin of the paper,
the open pores taking in the tinctures
swelling to smooth satiety until it
can't take anything additional in and
my brushes are dry again and have
given all they can, until we dip and
wash off in the other jar, we swish,
the faint colors swirling outward.

Metamorphosis

Because I am so large I have not yet wept
but my toes are curving in towards my soles.
I will be able to perch on a high round rod,
sway and look through the bars for you,
constantly turning so my peripheral eyes could scan.
I chew the seeds I am fed into a delicate pulp
stored as a sweet, tasty present for you.
My heart makes a continuous high-pitched noise
that reaches human ears as a mere sighing *ahhoooh*
but dogs hate to hear my ventricles screaming.
My teeth are gnashed now; forget capping them.
Without you, I would have no interest in my organs.
"Testicle" is just a snob's word for "short quiz."
I hope you can see my bright plumage and
respond to my woods-piercing cries.

Translation, 1

Sometimes I would give up this thick materiality
altogether, opt for the transmissible or subatomic,
just so I could meet with you silently, anytime,
anyplace, broadcast my love to you in electric
energy pods you receive and absorb, showering
down upon you through this gray day, golden and hot,
refulgent and fecund. *Enter, enter, miraculous lover!* you cry out,
your bedding askew, your arms akimbo, *I am receiving you
perfectly*, crackling, zipping sparks and sudden
temperature shifts and precipitation, and you
are fully awake and rapidly breathing and I feel
your fluttering and fluted pink organs, sense your musk,
while we leave in our wake the whole heavy world.

Translation, 2

Sometimes I slip from the aether, slithering
back to gnarled corporality as if my large feet
had the thick mud churned up on this swamped field
oozing between my knobby hammertoes. *Earthy*,
now that's the word, pebbles in my gizzard to digest
gallstones, kidney stones, roiling bones. I drink
ventis and grandes straight, no chaser, and poised
like a colossus let loose a thunderous cataract,
a fertilizing fount in the desert, reanimating the planet.
I lie down on your legs and face north, so beautiful,
this view way, this panorama, the vista opening before me.
Seismographs register my tectonic plates, our sliding,
the magma flows, north, further north, my fingers,
south my mouth and athletic plunge of the tongue.
Inside, I don't want to leave you for a moment, ever,
even if we must walk four-legged and enwrapped.

Dried Fruit on Ben Yehuda Street

If you held two large dried figs in your open palm
(thumb up, fingers in a relaxed curl),
you would certainly think of me. You'd note
something familiar in the deeply-lined,
brown-tan mottled outer skin, thick,
pliable, unexpectedly soft. You'd bounce them
in one hand and with the other,
play with the woody stem and excite
the multitude of seeds inside.
Dates make me think of you, small,
slim, their brown uniform and aureole.
Figs are primitive and thick; you
can chew around their fringes,
but each half of a date is a nipple.
I suck them gently for the sweetness and
they feel firmer, giving their sugar.
After, whether figs or dates,
all the fingers are sticky
and slick.

Dead Sea

I am an inverted jellyfish. My long toes and fingers
dangle lazily above the sea-soup. The bathing suit
bellows, puffs outwards, inwards, upwards.
Surface tension, minerals, coral reefs of salt,
my head bobbing magnetic north, soles southerly,
arms flat, back flat. The center of my compass rose
points to you, lying back, looking at your sky,
coinciding exactly with my latitude, you
standing under the spray of your shower
while I float in a hot sea the color of your eyes.

Busloads of Brazilians and wispy arthritics
turn into golems with the black mud. Alone
I build up surface tension dowsing for you,
the only living organism in this sea.

Winter Drive to Pullman

1. Eltopia

Sleet splattered, expressionist abstracts.
I recall you sheltering
in the rain-shadow of my beard.
I think of your kiss on my neck
and I swerve across the line,
the studded tires snare drums.

2. Dusty, Hay, Albion

The drenched cows, dark and sullen,
are so many Mafiosi at a graveside,
while the brown and white horses
wave their heads at each other,
waggle their legs and tails, tippsily carrying
their greigers and Mordechai masks
home from the synagogue.

But look:
the llamas on the hills of Albion
are fallen coconuts washed onto the beach.

3. Near Washtucna

Fresh green graffiti iridescent
on the frosty rough hillocks of rocks.
People stop to leave these signs
despite the legal warnings because
they yearn for their loves far away,
because they cannot do anything else,
because their hearts howl in the falling snow.

Night Vision

Before I died, when we still saw each other,
I cared about energy and vision, the news,
what was the new music, the talk of the critics,
even war and global warming. Now, doctors
would find me stuffed with dust and burlap,
skillfully preserved. My fever was tremendous;
I need your body to lock into my antibodies,
for I am Beloved-Positive. I have Acquired
Beloved-Deficiency Disorder. I have blocked the windows,
carefully coated my bedroom walls with ten coats
of black paint, and prepared a Nocturama,
my new post-life habitat. I have posted
informational poems on our love and sent tickets
only to you, my sole audience, my soul companion.
Come to me any night, here in the dark, and see
my eyes become much larger and glowing and moist,
watching for you as I hang from my trees
and make my plaintive mating calls to you
beneath the artful moon, like the one you brought
for both of us that night on the riverbank.

Yiddish for Travellers

I bought the book optimistically,
thinking to go there one day, to that lost land
where the border guards only know Yiddish,
where you hold out your passport and say,
"Awt iz mein pas. Tsee muz ich alts ayfennen?"
Must I open everything? And they let you pass,
you are okay with them. At the Post Office
you buy stamps engraved with fuzzy portraits
of Jacob Glatstein and Itzik Manger,
postcards of Mani Leib and Boris Tomashevsky.
The villages are all picturesque shtetls, you can
arrange for a tour by carriage and pass some nights
in centuries-old, thick-timbered shuls.
People gather to watch flickering black and white films
like *Green Fields* and *Die Meshugener*, and to
kvell whenever the lists of Nobel Prize winners
are published, to analyze the names and hab naches from the Jews.
Stay a long time; you can always go to a Yiddish bank and change
your dollars into the Yiddish money, or you say,
"Ich hab reisencheckn," and they take the traveler's check.
In the capitol of the Yiddish country, there are
shiny green, blue, and yellow trolleys, broad plazas
with delis and patisseries where the small tables
are filled with people reading and arguing and joking
over their strudel and rugelach, sipping tea in glasses.
They place sugar cubes in their mouths; they love herring.
They squeeze plump cheeks of nephews and grandchildren.
The people there are all oddly reminiscent of my relatives,
my aunts and uncles and great-aunts and great uncles,
and all of their relatives who I never met, who never
somehow crossed over, who were isolated perhaps
into this landlocked Yiddish land, where the police

speak Yiddish, where everyone is in terrific health,
vigorous and sometimes portly from all the pastries,
from the lack of stress, from having escaped
everything so thoroughly.

Ritual Baths

The ruins take on a certain sameness, the same
tan stones and dust, the rounded, worn steps,
the same sauna heat transforming tourists
into sun-dried tomatoes, shards and bones.

I always keep up with the guide and hear
same narratives again and again, until I
can guess in advance the ruins of the palace,
the Crusader add-ons, the Byzantine,

I can tell the store-rooms and tombs, the
ossuaries and aqueducts, the hippodrome,
the frigidarium, the tepidarium. In Masada,
at Miriam's palace, I study the mosaic floors

leading to the mikveh, the ritual bath, open
to two thousand years of dust and cloudless sky.
Guides give their spiel about the mikvehs, baths
and cisterns in Qumran, Akko, Tiberias,

below the Old City, everywhere there were
people bathing, and I think every time of you,
you in the first bath we shared, deep and foamy,
with powerful jets of water, a bottle of champagne,

I think of you bathing with me and without me,
I think of you bathing on the other side of the world,
I think of how your hair feels when I apply shampoo,
I think how pure and light we become, how we float.

Scroll

In the pink twilight after the tropical storm
I walk outside hearing dripping from every direction,
from every bent branch and dark frond,
the pink and gray and golden lights
reflected in the pools on the asphalt. Thunder
rumbles roll somewhere around the navel.

I am inside a long painting on rice paper;
let me explain it to you. The last element added
is the first seen. The red block in the corner with
such elegant calligraphic characters is the artist's sign.
It is from the Sung Dynasty, just after the great
epoch of vocal music, much like the Sixties. It
was followed by the Tang Dynasty, characterized
by powdered instant fruit drinks.

I am at the very bottom of the long scroll,
a long orange scrawl near the red signature block.
I am the sole figure there near the margin, just
above the faded purple mat, the fragile bamboo,
the muggy Atlantic ocean. You are at the top
in the far left hand corner, with layers of misty
green mountains, pine trees, flowing rivers,
waterfalls, azaleas, tea plants, acacias,
chittering insects and clicking frogs, sad-voiced birds.
You wear a silk kimono in bright blue paisleys,
a white obi, a seaglass necklace you touch
as you sip an incongruous vodka. You listen to your
pets, those caged crickets, those little dogs,
and gaze into the dark sky, the pinks and grays.

Between us through the old scroll so many

layers of ink and the allusion of distance is created
by added water for the far-away at the top,
bright full inks of black and red at the bottom.
There are such sharp cliffs and steep roads,
so many crags and impossible descents,
rocks piled from avalanches, bridges
torn from their moorings by floods.

I spend my days dreaming of you and writing to you.
That is why I am so pale and furrowed, my long beard
dipping dangerously close to the inkstones
and the wells where I mix my inks. I send you
scrolls daily with the first messenger going north,
to that distant left quarter of the known world.
I fill my thin characters with love; I thicken my inks
with passion, I make blushes of color with awe.
I tremble with adoration and recall.

The scroll captures all of the different stages of the journey
from here to there, over all those narrow, rocky paths,
around those bear-filled woods, across wild waters.
Here is the messenger at my door, a man in gray with wide hat,
picking up yesterday's scroll. There about a fifth of the way up,
a few inches left, a train a small wagons carry freight, including
last week's scrolls. Almost in the center, scrolls from two weeks ago
are in that ferry being pulled by teams of oxen. Then
things become misty. The scrolls are harder to track.
There are no notes from you arriving in return.

Do my scrolls every get there, to the far north?
Are they piled up in some closet in your distant rambling home?
Did they make you excited and happy, imagining
what I have imagined, recalling what I recall?
Every day I go sit outside on a bench to watch

for the messengers walking the path southeast to this town.
I am thrilled as long as I have hope that day of an answer.

I go back in with the rains and mix my inks and feel
faded, faded with each infusion of water, faded with days.

Year's End

Winter is nothing to me.
I already have an Antarctica in my heart.
My smallest internal spaces,
no longer warmed and nourished
by your hands or lips, have
rocky canyons, dusty riverbeds,
arroyos of bones. Not feeling
our shared breaths, my
lungs hold tundras and Saharas,
Ice Age rubble grates the
Great Plains of my brain.
We are about to have the year's
largest full moon. Do you remember
the real record-holder you gave me
as we held each other by the river's edge?
I have the full moon now coolly glowing
reflecting my fond thoughts of you,
my love, my sun, my source.

Jamming

Your day is too crowded to jam
me in. Try; squeeze me dry,
sweeten me with your sugar,
heat me and float on my aromas.
Jam me, my roller-derby *toughissima*,
my wild girl, or else let's jam
at the all-night jazz bar,
our faces dripping melted butter
from the brass instruments,
flashing jewels, liquor, crystal and ice,
the sweating, puff-cheeked faces
and opaque sunglasses.
Let me be your strawberries in season;
find me Friday in the farmers' market.
I am ripe for you; harvest my bushels,
peel and boil me, steam, stir me in the pot,
sprinkle me with flaxseed meal, taste
my vital gluten, shape me sweetly with your
fingers, form me with heat, bake me,
check my rising, spread over me with jam,
take me under your tongue and just
leave me to melt into your bloodstream.

Rooms

I wait for you here in these rooms
which are so ironically packed,
the unseen paintings stacked against walls,
with the books and papers, your image
everywhere I can place it. There
is no room in the rooms and yet
too much space. I rattle around
and spruce them up in case you visit.
I remind myself of *The Birdman
of Alcatraz*, of *The Man in the Iron Mask*.
I practice other languages, loudly
mispronouncing freely. I say "room"
with rolled r and aspirated h, *Rhooom*.
You should come to my *chambres, Zimmer*,
to hear me, *sh'ma* o love! I do best
with the silent letters and low
gutturals, and elisions. I wait for you
and listen only to the radio,
hearing miraculous things I want
to tell you; I can't save them all up.
I may hear of a surgical procedure
where they remove the heart entirely
(don't worry, my love, they use anesthesia,
I am sure and doesn't that word sound
like a place to go for a vacation?). The
empty space they fill with my unread
notes to you, wadded and shredded,
so I will look whole beneath the suture.
The heart has two chambers, as well:
auricle must be related to ear or to
Orricle and oral and longs for your voice;
ventricle has the icy wind blowing through

and moans with each opening and closing.
The removed heart, still beating, I'll
have sewn to my shirt above the left elbow.
You'll be able to see it at a distance
and perhaps you'll be tempted close, maybe
come over and give it a squeeze.

Personal Ad

I want a woman who will wrap herself so tightly around my back our ribs will interlace like shuffled cards; I want her to grip me so tenaciously, she will never slip away.

I want a woman who will squeeze my soul directly into her veins so she becomes addicted to me, as I am to her.

I want a woman so attuned to music she takes it in not with her ears but three inches below her navel; those notes and vibrations send heat down to her thighs then under and around to tingle in the dimples of her back. O, those soaring licks!

I want a woman who tattoos my back with her strong fingers, the ten small purplish indentations marking the place for the pinions of my angelic wings.

I want a language-drunk woman who will make me kick my serifs off, mess up my gray Times Roman, persuade my bones to incline into Garamond *italics*, let me loll playfully in her pink Helvetica, and suddenly bloom into **bold**.

I want a woman who will lead me away, who will grab me by my scruff and insist, *Now!* No matter where or when or what; *Now!* I know her instincts are always right.

I want no substitute woman, no artificial ingredient woman, no soggy, weak-willed, low-fiber woman. I want a tongue-thrilling, tasty, organic woman. I just want you, the woman I knew, just you, just you, just you.

Understanding the Rocks

1. Slowly, slowly

Gifts from you, my guru. I am studying them.
The rocks I see now are to teach me patience.
Im—
        mense
                pa—
                        tience.

Nights I sit up to confront the rocks,
to catch them changing. I strive to deserve you.

I wait alone   for the   rocks
to change.   Alone I wait for
the rocks   to change.   I
wait for the   rocks alone to
change.   I wait for the rocks
to change alone. I alone wait
for   the rocks   to change.
I wait alone   for the   rocks
to change.   Alone I wait for
the rocks   to change.   I
wait for the   rocks alone to
change.   I wait for the rocks
to change alone. I alone wait
for   the rocks   to change.
I wait alone   for the   rocks
to change.   Alone I wait for
the rocks   to change.   I
wait for the   rocks alone to
change.   I wait for the rocks
to change alone. I alone wait

for   the rocks   to change.

You must realize
the rocks will change
before I do.

2. The Bag

The rocks tease through the gold cloth.
I can imagine your smile when the rocks
slid from your hand into the open bag,
knocking gently against each other,
klik clic qliq ngugsz, featherweight boulders.

Tell me how you selected the bag;
what did you intend? The gold mesh
hides and shows the gray seastones.
Net, nest, *cache-sexe*, pouch, pocket,
snugly bound with gold ribbon.

Did you roll the rocks around in the sack
(let's be the rocks rolling around in the sack),
squeezing, releasing your grip? I feel and see you
through the thin silks, the sheer and translucent,
the shimmering, the white, you, not the rocks.

3. Origins

I hold the rocks in my palm
vertically, veined towers,
five primitive erect stacks,

a private Rockhenge.
Here I will bring you
offerings of oil and grain,
splash my words seven times,
spatter the ground and walls
with my chants of praise.

The rocks click in place
one by one on the nightstand.
The grain of the wood
recalls the gray beach where
you found these stones for me.
After my room is dark and cold
I hear the water washing the rocks,
spumes and foam and lunar tides
in and out, smoother and smoother.

The water washes around your feet
as you stand in the water selecting
these exact stones, then washes around
your thighs and hands as you bend,
guided to these, thinking of me.
I taste the salt on your skin, I
nudge and poke into the rocks,
in and out together, lunar tides
and solar winds, all forces
bringing us in and out,
in and out.

4. Pressure and Stress

What is their type, these rocks? You

sent some private, coded message
of love or critique to me, who
is an absolute geologic virgin,
a blank slate until you inscribe me.

Surely we are metamorphic, our
open pores flecked with sillimanite and garnet,
sparkly olivines and feldspar. O love,
to be sedimentary with you through
still eons, relaxing as our strata cooled.

You can still hug me with such force
my mica forms those dark bands
and you delight at my foliation, my
gneissosity. I adore your slaty cleavage,
my love, my sweet quartz-porphyry.

5. Sedimentary

Those rare nesting weekends
we were served strata.
They were such sedimentary days,
we stretched in layers,
you, me, you, me.

Permeated with magma,
you fill my thick joints,
the planes of bedding.

6. Large Rock

Naturally I empathized with the largest rock,
the clumsy oddball among the small, sexy stones.
It would be waved by the photographers
to stand way in the back (*keep going, keep going!*)
among the misshaped broken chalk cliffs
instead of with you among the others in front.
The largest rock is left-handed, near-sighted,
rigid, of course, a strange rock, sensitive to cold,
dreamless through lonely nights, weeks, months.
The largest rock is the only one of the set
with holes (it probably jokes it is holy, it is
a Jewish rock, it laughs silently, or it may
laugh with deep rumbling, only there are
no beautiful rocks near enough to hear). Tell me,
slim rock, smooth young rock, rock of my
endless, dreamless nights, how do you
interpret these? What forces shaped these
tunnels carved into the heart of the largest rock?
One tunnel goes straight through like a suicide's bullet
but the other stops halfway and hidden there
is a wave-formed pebble, like you inside me
since the Big Bang, since the start of time.

7. Flat

The two smallest rocks are just beginning
to yield their meanings, to pass to me
your whispered messages. These two
are shaped alike for reasons, but different in
color, thickness, smoothness. Clearly

(not that things are clear with rocks!),
the beautiful gray-green rock, the ultimate
in my collection, stands for you. It is
perfect, flawless and thin, desirable
from any angle, my angel. I see that you
intend the other rock, with its dark color,
oxidized and worn purple, to be me. It is
marked by some rugged pitting that
can be defended in view of its age,
its travels from volcanic cones through oceans
to the place you found it stranded;
you would tell me it is a handsome rock.
The concave dark disk fits my thumb
as my thumb fits your pelvis, as it fits
your supersternal notch, or those two
dimples at the end of your spine. The
small rock accepts your finer thumb
that has plumbed all of my crannies.
Both rocks have been worn down as
worry stones, for our thumbs to circle
and roll and rub and press during
all those times we are not together.
They are like prayerwheels, rosaries,
Tibetan paper flags ripped by winds
in icy passes, they are like tefillin
and tztzis, they are reminders of
our absent other, they are to keep us
hopeful and calm, smiling within.

8. Fused

I only came to see through its effects
that the last rock was meant to cheer me,

to boost my spirits when you are away.
I left it out these last two weeks to
regard it closely in every light and time.
It has become a one-and-a-quarter inch
Prozac, a Chinese herbalist's confection,
the chewy honeycomb candy of my youth,
"Seafoam," so aptly named (you spotting
this stone in the roiling, bubbly shallows,
plucking this one, out of the millions;
you are my Aphrodite, my doctor, my all).
I left the rock untouched until today,
watching it in cloudlight, in dazzling sun,
in incandescence, seeming to reveal
your warm intentions. I surprised the rock
in the dark, but it did not jump; it remained
still, stiller than still, and it is still still.
It became fuzzed with a dusty halo. It is
smooth to the touch while rough for the eye.
Curved and flat, striated and scarred, half
graytan and half grayblue, it's obvious
this was originally two entirely separate stones
flung by cosmic forces from distant stars
or shot out into the stratosphere by volcanoes,
each to whirl about in search of the other; their
fusion was never in doubt for a moment.
When they joined, making this joyous whole stone
from two long-searching halves, Vesuvius
and Mount St. Helen's rumbled with relief
and celebratory magma flowed again. Rocks
have patience, rocks can withstand long waiting.
Now young limestone hopes as it drips fervently
and granite wants its torn edges worn smooth,
and this beautiful mixed and concentrated rock
cheers me as I wait for you, unchanging love.

Perenniel

Now that Spring has finally taken hold,
I want to do for you
what the sun does for the Earth.
However far apart we are,
in space terms we are pressed tightly together.
I want you to feel my rays daily
melt your resisting ice crystals
and send the overflow from foggy
snow-packed mountain crevices
flowing down to your feet.
I want you to overflow, to flood,
to breech your levies. I want to wash
over your parched plains
and have your fill of drink
until you thirst no more.
I want to make your sap run
and make you join in our spawning
cycles set before time.
Race upstream to be with me
no matter what, no matter
those dams and locks and mountains.
Such puny obstacles for us
when it is Spring, after all.
I want you to bud, to flower,
to do the dance of the cambium flow,
to send out new shoots, pollen,
such heady aromas and rhizomes,
to turn all your new surfaces
to face my heat through the lengthening days.

Unfurl those sweet leaves of yours,
let me land gently in your green fresh cells.
Let's make some sugar and give away oxygen.
Let's throw off the winter together.

Leonard Orr is Academic Director of Liberal Arts and Professor of English at the Tri-Cities campus of Washington State University. He is the author or editor of thirteen books of literary criticism or critical theory. His most recent books are *Joyce, Imperialism, and Postcolonialism* (Syracuse University Press, 2008), and *Henry James's The Turn of the Screw* (Continuum, 2009). He was named the Lewis E. and Stella G. Buchanan Distinguished Professor of English (2005-08).

His poetry has appeared in many journals including *Black Warrior Review, Fugue, Poetry International, Poetry East, Natural Bridge, Isotope, Midwest Poetry Review, Pontoon, Rosebud,* and *Rocky Mountain Review*. His poetry chapbook, *Daytime Moon*, was published in 2005 by FootHills Press. He was a finalist for the T. S. Eliot Poetry Prize and the Blue Lynx Poetry Prize and was a semifinalist for the Floating Bridge Chapbook Prize and the William Stafford Poetry Prize. He has been a featured reader in many venues throughout the state, and he has led poetry workshops at the Burning Word Poetry Festival and elsewhere. He hosts the open mic and featured poet events at Washington State University Tri-Cities and served as president of the Washington Poets Association for three years. In recent years, he has taken up painting abstracts and had his work featured in a solo-exhibition of fifty paintings in 2007. Both his poetry and painting utilize a similar aesthetic based in spontaneity, surprise, and passion.